Wow! Smart Vocabulary

4

워크북

Unit 1

Personality

Word Check

Ⓐ 다음 단어들의 우리말 뜻을 모두 알고 있나요? 확인해 보세요.

> 단어의 품사에 맞는 우리말 뜻을 쓰세요.

1. ☐ everyone 대
2. ☐ personality 명
3. ☐ shy 형
4. ☐ careful 형
5. ☐ practical 형
6. ☐ focus 동 / 명
7. ☐ goal 명
8. ☐ end 명
9. ☐ social 형
10. ☐ give up 구
11. ☐ both 형
12. ☐ responsible 형

13. ☐ classmate 명
14. ☐ awful 형
15. ☐ selfish 형
16. ☐ borrow 동
17. ☐ naughty 형
18. ☐ answer 동 / 명
19. ☐ tease 동
20. ☐ complain 동
21. ☐ like 동 / 전
22. ☐ kid 명
23. ☐ others 명
24. ☐ tough 형

Ⓑ 우리말과 같은 뜻이 되도록 빈칸을 채워 영어 문장을 완성하세요.

1.	모든 사람들은 혈액형이 있다.	_____ has a blood type.
2.	혈액형은 성격에 영향을 끼친다고 여겨진다.	Your blood type is believed to influence your _____.
3.	혈액형이 A형인 사람들은 부끄러움을 타고 긴장을 잘한다.	People with blood type A are _____ and nervous.

4.	그들은 매우 신중하다.	They are very _____ .
5.	혈액형이 B형인 사람들은 대단히 현실적이다.	Blood type B people are very _____ .
6.	그들은 무언가를 할 때 그것에 집중한다.	When they do something, they _____ on it.
7.	그들은 자신들의 목표에 도달하려고 열심히 노력한다.	They try hard to reach their _____ .
8.	그리고 그들은 끝까지 열심히 한다.	And they work hard to the _____ .
9.	혈액형이 O형인 사람들은 외향적이고 사교적이다.	People with blood type O are outgoing and _____ .
10.	그들은 또 쉽게 포기한다.	They also _____ _____ easily.
11.	혈액형이 AB형인 사람들은 소심하기도 하면서 외향적이기도 하다.	Blood type AB people are _____ timid and outgoing.
12.	AB형 사람들은 책임감이 있다.	AB type people are _____ .
13.	"너의 새로운 반 친구들은 어땠니?"	"How were your new _____ ?"
14.	"그들은 끔찍해요!"	"They are _____ !"
15.	"짝꿍인 저스틴은 매우 이기적이에요."	"My partner Justin is very _____ ."
16.	"내가 연필을 빌려달라고 하니까 싫다고 했어요."	"He said no when I asked to _____ a pencil."
17.	"매튜는 장난이 심해요."	"Matthew is _____ ."
18.	"내가 수업 시간에 틀린 답을 말했어요."	"I gave the wrong _____ in class."
19.	"그러니까, 그애가 나를 놀렸어요."	"Then, he _____ me."
20.	"그레이스는 계속 불평을 해요."	"Grace _____ over and over."
21.	"엄마, 나는 이 학교가 정말 싫어요."	"Mom, I really don't _____ this school."
22.	"나는 좋은 아이가 있을 거라고 믿는단다."	"I'm sure there is a good _____ ."
23.	"아, 미셸이라는 여자 아이는 다른 아이들과 달랐어요."	"Ah, a girl named Michelle was different from the _____ ."
24.	"첫 날은 항상 힘들단다."	"It's always _____ on the first day."

Review Test

A 빈칸에 어울리는 단어를 고르세요.

1. Don't act like a _____. You're 20 years old.
   ① fast   ② flat   ③ kid   ④ animal

2. Do you have math or science today? I have _____ of them.
   ① reach   ② both   ③ record   ④ three

3. My classmates are _____. They don't listen to our teacher.
   ① full   ② empty   ③ bricks   ④ naughty

4. My doctor says that my sister can't do ballet anymore. She has
   to _____ ballet.
   ① like   ② make   ③ give up   ④ start

5. She _____ me about my hairstyle.
   ① teases   ② swallows   ③ swings   ④ thinks

6. He is _____, so he never speaks in class.
   ① supporting   ② shy   ③ suffering   ④ studying

7. Tom tried hard to achieve his _____, but he failed.
   ① corner   ② skirt   ③ goal   ④ gift

8. She never shares her food. She is _____.
   ① sail   ② selfish   ③ say   ④ severe

9. Everybody, give me your attention. _____ on me, please.
   ① Ready   ② Get tired   ③ Get some rest ④ Focus

10. A _____ girl is so strong that she can fight a boy.
    ① weak   ② dry   ③ expensive   ④ tough

11. Dynamite can explore easily. You must be _____.
    ① careful   ② strange   ③ happy   ④ sleepy

12. I need to call my mom, but I don't have a phone. Can I _____ yours?

    ① date   ② borrow   ③ build   ④ dirty

13. The movie is really exciting from beginning to _____.

    ① exit   ② great   ③ green   ④ end

14. Don't _____. There is nothing I can do.

    ① clean   ② complain   ③ bring   ④ branch

15. That's my fault. I am _____ for the problem.

    ① responsible   ② speak   ③ respectful   ④ spread

B 밑줄 친 단어와 비슷한 뜻을 가진 단어를 고르세요.

16. Good morning, <u>everyone</u>.

    ① lady   ② gentle man   ③ everybody   ④ cousin

17. He is my <u>classmate</u>.

    ① cry   ② friend   ③ teacher   ④ slippery

18. Tell me what his <u>personality</u> is like.

    ① ocean   ② slip   ③ character   ④ taste

C 밑줄 친 단어와 반대되는 뜻을 가진 단어를 고르세요.

19. Can you <u>answer</u> the question?

    ① solve   ② ask   ③ like   ④ close

20. I <u>like</u> seafood except for oysters.

    ① sharp   ② small   ③ large   ④ dislike

Score: _____ /20

Unit 2

A Swimming Race

Word Check

A 다음 단어들의 우리말 뜻을 모두 알고 있나요? 확인해 보세요.

단어의 품사에 맞는 우리말 뜻을 쓰세요.

1. ☐ take place	구		13. ☐ turtle	명	
2. ☐ block	명		14. ☐ run away	구	
3. ☐ that	접 대 형		15. ☐ toward	전	
4. ☐ signal	명 동		16. ☐ than	접 전	
5. ☐ powerfully	부		17. ☐ splash	동	
6. ☐ do one's best	구		18. ☐ paddle	동	
7. ☐ neck and neck	구		19. ☐ get a cramp	구	
8. ☐ predict	동		20. ☐ left	형 명	
9. ☐ result	명		21. ☐ anymore	부	
10. ☐ catch up with	구		22. ☐ save	동	
11. ☐ second	명 형		23. ☐ lifesaver	명	
12. ☐ record	명 동		24. ☐ go back	구	

B 우리말과 같은 뜻이 되도록 빈칸을 채워 영어 문장을 완성하세요.

1.	400 미터 자유형 수영 경기가 지금 열리고 있다.	A 400 m freestyle swimming race is [ ] [ ] now.
2.	다섯 명의 수영 선수들이 출발대에 있다.	Five swimmers are at the starting [ ].
3.	우리는 팽팽한 경기가 될 것으로 예상한다.	We expect [ ] it will be a close race.

4.	수영 선수들이 출발 신호를 기다리고 있다.	The swimmers are waiting for the starting _____.
5.	그들은 힘차게 수영을 하고 있다.	They are swimming _____.
6.	다섯 명의 수영 선수들이 모두 최선을 다한다.	All five swimmers _____.
7.	그들은 막상막하로 수영을 하고 있다.	They are swimming _____.
8.	우리는 이 경기에서 누가 이길지 예측할 수가 없다.	We cannot _____ who will win this race.
9.	우리는 아직 이 시합의 결과들을 모른다.	We don't know the _____ of this race yet.
10.	에릭이 다른 수영 선수들을 따라잡는다.	Eric _____ the other swimmers.
11.	그는 3분 58초로 끝낸다.	He finishes in 3 minutes 58 _____.
12.	이것은 신기록이다.	It's a new _____.
13.	닉과 그의 친구들은 해변에서 거북이 한 마리를 발견했다.	Nick and his friends found a _____ at the beach.
14.	닉은 그것을 잡으려고 했지만 그것은 그에게서 도망쳤다.	Nick tried to catch it, but it _____ from him.
15.	그것은 서둘러서 바다를 향해 빨리 움직였다.	It hurried and moved quickly _____ the sea.
16.	그것은 닉보다 더 빨리 수영을 했다.	It swam faster _____ Nick.
17.	저스틴이 소리쳤다. "닉, 물에서 첨벙거려."	Justin shouted, "Nick, _____ in the water."
18.	그레이스가 소리쳤다. "손으로 물장구를 쳐."	Grace shouted, "_____ with your hands."
19.	갑자기 그의 발에 쥐가 났다.	Suddenly, he _____ in his foot.
20.	그는 왼쪽 발을 움직일 수 없었다.	He couldn't move his _____ foot.
21.	그래서 그는 더 이상 수영할 수가 없었다.	So he couldn't swim _____.
22.	"나를 구해줘서 고마워."	"Thank you for _____ me."
23.	"너는 생명의 은인이야."	"You are a _____."
24.	그것은 웃으며 바다로 돌아갔다.	It smiled and _____ into the sea.

Review Test

A 빈칸에 어울리는 단어를 고르세요.

1. When I fell into the lake, Mike saved me. He is a _____.
   ① record   ② sign   ③ lifesaver   ④ outcome

2. Ann doesn't live here _____.
   ① anymore   ② that   ③ some more   ④ long

3. I _____ in my leg, so I couldn't walk alone.
   ① got to   ② caught up with   ③ result   ④ got a cramp

4. Do you know the _____ of the election?
   ① save   ② repeat   ③ second   ④ result

5. He wanted to win the game, so he _____.
   ① did his best   ② had luck   ③ fail   ④ block

6. I am faster _____ my friends. I always win the running races.
   ① when   ② than   ③ that   ④ then

7. A bird flies _____ a big tree.
   ① in   ② going   ③ toward   ④ through

8. After the runner fell over, he couldn't run _____.
   ① powerful   ② strong   ③ signal   ④ powerfully

9. You have to check the traffic _____ before crossing the road.
   ① sing   ② signal   ③ splash   ④ block

10. They said _____ they had lost their cat at the park.
    ① that   ② than   ③ what   ④ which

11. It was not possible to _____ the other runners.
    ① come into   ② think   ③ buy   ④ catch up with

8

12. I want to have a _____ for a pet.
   ① truck   ② turtle   ③ paddle   ④ power

13. He has a great _____ as a swimmer.
   ① record   ② second   ③ react   ④ plant

14. I ran _____ with him.
   ① alone   ② neck and neck   ③ block   ④ from

15. I can run 100 meters in 15 _____. I'm fast.
   ① hours   ② minutes   ③ times   ④ seconds

B 밑줄 친 단어와 비슷한 뜻을 가진 단어를 고르세요.

16. The next singing contest will <u>take place</u> in our city.
   ① take a break   ② hold   ③ be held   ④ take a chance

17. Can you <u>predict</u> what will happen in the future?
   ① prepare   ② forecast   ③ step   ④ net

18. We have to <u>go back</u> to our country.
   ① return   ② go camping   ③ rewrite   ④ repeat

19. The rabbit <u>ran away</u> from the tiger.
   ① jumped   ② fought   ③ saved   ④ escaped

C 밑줄 친 단어와 반대되는 뜻을 가진 단어를 고르세요.

20. Go straight and turn <u>left</u> at the corner.
   ① next   ② back   ③ right   ④ front

Score: _____ /20

Unit 3
The Tallest Building

Word Check

Ⓐ 다음 단어들의 우리말 뜻을 모두 알고 있나요? 확인해 보세요.

> 단어의 품사에 맞는 우리말 뜻을 쓰세요.

1. ☐ welcome	동			13. ☐ tornado	명		
2. ☐ skyscraper	명			14. ☐ into	전		
3. ☐ tall	형			15. ☐ order	동	명	
4. ☐ height	명			16. ☐ brick	명		
5. ☐ steel	명			17. ☐ quickly	부		
6. ☐ strong	형			18. ☐ heaven	명		
7. ☐ company	명			19. ☐ stone	명		
8. ☐ million	명	형		20. ☐ storm	명		
9. ☐ observation	명			21. ☐ collapse	동		
10. ☐ sway	동			22. ☐ dust	명		
11. ☐ city	명			23. ☐ floor	명		
12. ☐ skyline	명			24. ☐ destroy	동		

Ⓑ 우리말과 같은 뜻이 되도록 빈칸을 채워 영어 문장을 완성하세요.

1.	시카고의 시어스 타워에 오신 것을 환영합니다.	_____ to the Sears Tower in Chicago.
2.	저는 이 유명한 고층 빌딩의 가이드 테드입니다.	I'm Ted, a guide for this famous _____.
3.	이것은 세계에서 가장 높은 빌딩 중 하나입니다.	This is one of the _____ buildings in the world.

4.	이것의 높이는 약 440 미터입니다.	Its _____ is about 440 meters.
5.	이것은 강철로 만들어졌습니다.	It is made of _____.
6.	이것은 110층을 떠받치기에 충분히 강합니다.	It is _____ enough to support 110 stories.
7.	여기에는 백여 개 이상의 회사가 들어서 있습니다.	It is home to more than 100 _____.
8.	해마다 백 삼십만 명의 관광객들이 스카이덱을 방문합니다.	Every year, 1.3 _____ tourists visit the Skydeck.
9.	여기가 전망대입니다.	Here is the _____ deck.
10.	이 바람 부는 날 빌딩이 흔들리는 것을 느끼시나요?	Can you feel how the building _____ on this windy day?
11.	도시 멀리와 미시건 호수 너머가 보이시나요?	Can you see far over the _____ and across Lake Michigan?
12.	시카고의 지평선은 정말 멋지답니다.	The Chicago _____ is so wonderful.
13.	토네이도가 갑자기 나타난다.	A _____ suddenly appears.
14.	그것은 닉을 그림 속으로 데려간다.	It takes Nick _____ the picture.
15.	어떤 사람들이 지푸라기로 벽돌들을 만들고 있다.	Some people are making _____ out of straw.
16.	감독관은 닉에게 명령을 내린다.	A director gives an _____ to Nick.
17.	한 노인이 "어서, 그것들을 그냥 빨리 끌고 와."라고 말한다.	An old man says, "Come on. Just drag them _____."
18.	"이 탑은 하늘까지 높이 올라 갈 거야."	"The tower will go high up into the _____."
19.	닉은 "어, 안돼요. 그것을 떠받칠 강한 돌과 나무가 필요해요."라고 말한다.	Nick says, "Oh, no. You need strong _____ and wood to support it."
20.	폭풍이 강하게 불어온다.	A _____ is blowing angrily.
21.	탑은 연기 구름 속에서 무너진다.	The tower _____ in a cloud of smoke.
22.	사람들은 비명을 지르며 먼지로 뒤덮인다.	People scream and are covered in _____.
23.	닉은 그림에서 마룻바닥으로 떨어진다.	Nick drops down on the _____ from the picture.
24.	이제, 바벨탑은 파괴되었다.	Now, the Tower of Babel is _____.

Review Test

A 빈칸에 어울리는 단어를 고르세요.

1. My house is behind the bank. It's a _____ house.
   ① bride ② bread ③ brick ④ break

2. My dad is busy. He runs a _____.
   ① compass ② company ③ computer ④ complaint

3. It's a huge building. It's the tallest _____ in the world.
   ① skyline ② skyscraper ③ skylark ④ skydiving

4. The _____ is getting worse. We can't go camping.
   ① story ② storm ③ store ④ stove

5. This bridge is safe. _____ poles support it.
   ① Street ② Still ③ Steal ④ Steel

6. Many students visit this museum. About 3 _____ come every year.
   ① millimeter ② million ③ minute ④ military

7. The wind is blowing. The branches are _____.
   ① switching ② swimming ③ swaying ④ sweeping

8. You're very tall. What's your _____?
   ① health ② heavy ③ height ④ helmet

9. I'm really _____ books. Sometimes I read all day.
   ① with ② into ③ up ④ out

10. He threw a _____ and broke the window.
    ① stone ② start ③ storm ④ study

11. I'm very _____. Let's wrestle.
    ① strong ② street ③ strike ④ strap

12. I messed up the room. My mother _____ me to clean up.
　① agreed　　② arranged　　③ organized　　④ ordered

13. We had heavy rain, so the roof _____.
　① collapsed　　② collected　　③ controlled　　④ compared

14. _____ to our show. This is the best show in the world.
　① Wear　　② Weather　　③ Wonder　　④ Welcome

15. The desk is covered in _____. Clean it up.
　① dream　　② duty　　③ dust　　④ dash

B 밑줄 친 단어와 비슷한 뜻을 가진 단어를 고르세요.

16. We are leaving the <u>city</u>. It's too noisy.
　① building　　② town　　③ country　　④ farm

17. This building has 100 <u>floors</u>. It's very tall.
　① elevators　　② stories　　③ steps　　④ nets

C 밑줄 친 단어와 반대되는 뜻을 가진 단어를 고르세요.

18. A tornado hit our city. It <u>destroyed</u> many buildings.
　① trapped　　② ruined　　③ changed　　④ constructed

19. Mom is coming. Clean your room <u>quickly</u>.
　① hardly　　② sadly　　③ slowly　　④ highly

20. My mom is very <u>tall</u>. She is taller than my dad.
　① high　　② low　　③ short　　④ large

Score: _____ /20

Unit 4

Paper World

Word Check

A 다음 단어들의 우리말 뜻을 모두 알고 있나요? 확인해 보세요.

단어의 품사에 맞는 우리말 뜻을 쓰세요.

1. ☐ wetland ㉅
2. ☐ ancient ㉇
3. ☐ no ㉇ ㉈
4. ☐ ago ㉈
5. ☐ part ㉅
6. ☐ strip ㉅ ㉆
7. ☐ soak ㉆
8. ☐ then ㉈
9. ☐ sheet ㉅
10. ☐ sunlight ㉅
11. ☐ origin ㉅
12. ☐ century ㉅

13. ☐ art class ㉅
14. ☐ sketch ㉅ ㉆
15. ☐ erase ㉆
16. ☐ give out light ㉍
17. ☐ everything ㉎
18. ☐ realize ㉆
19. ☐ drawing paper ㉅
20. ☐ listen ㉆
21. ☐ wave ㉆ ㉅
22. ☐ look around ㉍
23. ☐ rub ㉆
24. ☐ pop out ㉍

B 우리말과 같은 뜻이 되도록 빈칸을 채워 영어 문장을 완성하세요.

1.	파피루스는 습지들에서 자라는 식물이다.	Papyrus is a plant which grows in the _____.
2.	그것은 고대 이집트인들에 의해서 사용되었다.	It was used by the _____ Egyptians.
3.	세상에 종이가 없었다면 하고 상상할 수 있는가?	Can you imagine if there was _____ paper in the world?

4.	이집트인들은 수 천년 전에 어떻게 종이를 만들었을까?	How did the Egyptians make paper thousands of years _____ ?
5.	그들은 파피루스 식물의 바깥 쪽 부분의 껍질을 벗겼다.	They peeled off the outer _____ of the papyrus plant.
6.	그들은 안쪽 부분을 얇고 가는 조각들로 잘랐다.	They cut the inner _____ into thin _____ .
7.	다음에 그들은 그것들을 물에 적셨다.	Next, they _____ them in water.
8.	그리고 나서, 무슨 일이 일어났다고 생각하는가?	_____ , what do you think happened?
9.	그들은 그것들을 평평하게 펴서 시트로 만들었다.	They flattened them into _____ .
10.	마지막으로, 그것들은 햇빛에 건조되었다.	Lastly, they were dried in _____ .
11.	'종이'라는 말의 기원은 '파피루스'에서 왔다.	The _____ of the word "paper" comes from "papyrus."
12.	파피루스는 8세기까지 사용되었다.	Papyrus was used until the 8th _____ .
13.	닉은 야외에서 미술 수업을 한다.	Nick has _____ outdoors.
14.	닉은 운동장에 있는 나무들과 놀이기구들을 스케치하고 있다.	Nick is _____ trees and rides in the playground.
15.	그는 큰 나무의 일부분을 지운다.	He _____ parts of a tall tree.
16.	그러자 나무가 빛을 낸다.	So, the tree _____ .
17.	그의 주변에 있는 모든 것들이 하얀색이다.	_____ around him is white.
18.	그는 자신이 종이 안에 있다는 것을 깨닫는다.	He _____ that he is in the paper.
19.	그는 도화지 밖으로 나가고 싶다.	He wants to get out of the _____ .
20.	닉은 큰 나무 위로 올라 가서 주변을 둘러본다.	Nick climbs up the tall tree and _____ .
21.	"여기 아무도 없어요? 내 말 좀 들어봐요!"	"Is anybody here? _____ to me!"
22.	닉이 소리치면서 손을 흔든다.	Nick shouts and _____ his hands.
23.	저스틴은 문을 그리고 그 종이를 문지른다.	Justin draws a door and _____ the paper.
24.	그러자, 문이 열리고 불쌍한 닉이 종이 밖으로 튀어나온다.	Then, the door opens, and poor Nick _____ _____ of the paper.

Review Test

A 빈칸에 어울리는 단어를 고르세요.

1. Different kinds of _____ and wildlife live in the wetlands.
   ① planes   ② plans   ③ plants   ④ plays

2. _____ man can fly, but birds can.
   ① Not   ② No   ③ Never   ④ Neither

3. Icebergs are huge. But they are just _____ of glaciers.
   ① parts   ② paths   ③ pants   ④ pans

4. The building was on fire last night. But the _____ of the fire is a mystery.
   ① outside   ② orange   ③ onion   ④ origin

5. In the 20th _____, there were two world wars. That changed the world forever.
   ① center   ② century   ③ ceremony   ④ ceiling

6. Make sure you bring some _____ and a pencil next time.
   ① drawing paper   ② dream   ③ door   ④ drink

7. I'm _____ the model. He's sitting very still on the chair.
   ① sketching   ② swimming   ③ shopping   ④ sleeping

8. Would you _____ my name from the list?
   ① extend   ② erase   ③ escape   ④ explain

9. A flashlight _____ in the dark. It's very useful.
   ① goes out   ② is dead   ③ gives out light   ④ is expensive

10. I got a health checkup. _____ is fine.
    ① Example   ② Excuse   ③ Event   ④ Everything

11. Gulliver _____ that he was in a mini world. He was too big for it.
    ① ran   ② rolled   ③ replied   ④ realized

12. We have _____ on Thursday. I like drawing and painting.
  ① English class   ② art class   ③ math class   ④ science class

13. There is a parade in the street. The president is _____ his hands.
  ① waving   ② waiting   ③ wanting   ④ wondering

14. _____ the lamp and make a wish.
  ① Rush   ② Rub   ③ Relax   ④ Regret

15. Santa Claus _____ of the card. It is called a pop-up card.
  ① points at   ② pulls over   ③ pops out   ④ puts on

16. My father _____ the back yard.
  ① looks for   ② looks around   ③ looks after   ④ looks like

B 밑줄 친 단어와 비슷한 뜻을 가진 단어를 고르세요.

17. He and I met just a few minutes <u>ago</u>.
  ① begin   ② behind   ③ before   ④ beat

18. Plants need enough <u>sunlight</u> to grow.
  ① sunrise   ② sunshine   ③ sunglasses   ④ sunburn

19. <u>Listen</u> to my words carefully and remember them.
  ① Happen   ② Hide   ③ Hear   ④ Hire

C 밑줄 친 단어와 반대되는 뜻을 가진 단어를 고르세요.

20. Seoul is also the <u>ancient</u> capital of the Joseon Dynasty.
  ① deep   ② dear   ③ dead   ④ modern

Score: _____ /20

Water Changes

Word Check

Ⓐ 다음 단어들의 우리말 뜻을 모두 알고 있나요? 확인해 보세요.

> 단어의 품사에 맞는 우리말 뜻을 쓰세요.

1. ☐ surface	명	
2. ☐ river	명	
3. ☐ heat	명 동	
4. ☐ water vapor	명	
5. ☐ rise	동	
6. ☐ up	부	
7. ☐ water drop	명	
8. ☐ form	명 동	
9. ☐ or	접	
10. ☐ flow	동	
11. ☐ down	부	
12. ☐ water cycle	명	

13. ☐ cover	명 동	
14. ☐ sheep	명	
15. ☐ ocean	명	
16. ☐ lighten	동	
17. ☐ turn into	구	
18. ☐ evaporate	동	
19. ☐ a lot of	구	
20. ☐ chilly	형	
21. ☐ each other	구	
22. ☐ freeze	동	
23. ☐ person	명	
24. ☐ cool	형	

Ⓑ 우리말과 같은 뜻이 되도록 빈칸을 채워 영어 문장을 완성하세요.

1. 지구 표면의 70 퍼센트는 물이다.

   70% of the Earth's _____ is water.

2. 태양은 강 위를 비춘다.

   The sun shines on the _____ .

3. 그것은 물을 데운다.

   It _____ the water.

4.	물은 수증기가 된다.	Water becomes _____ _____.
5.	그것은 강에서부터 올라간다.	It _____ from the river.
6.	그것은 하늘로 올라간다.	It goes _____ into the sky.
7.	그것은 차가워져서 물방울들이 된다.	It gets cold and becomes _____ _____.
8.	그것들은 함께 모여서 구름을 형성한다.	They come together and _____ clouds.
9.	그것들은 비나 눈으로 강으로 떨어진다.	They fall into the rivers as rain _____ snow.
10.	물은 상류에서 아래로 온다.	Water comes _____ from upper streams.
11.	강들은 바다로 흐른다.	The rivers _____ into the sea.
12.	물의 순환은 다시 시작한다.	The _____ begins again.
13.	하늘이 구름들로 덮여 있다.	The sky is _____ with clouds.
14.	구름들이 양떼처럼 생겼다.	The clouds look like a flock of _____.
15.	닉은 눈을 감고 바다에 있는 튜브 위에 누워 있다.	Nick closes his eyes and lies on a tube in the _____.
16.	닉은 몸이 가벼워지는 것을 느낀다.	Nick feels his body _____.
17.	눈을 뜨자 그가 물로 변한다.	When he opens his eyes, he _____ _____ water.
18.	그는 증발해서 하늘로 올라간다.	He _____ and goes _____ into the sky.
19.	그는 하늘에 많은 친구들이 있다.	He has _____ _____ friends in the sky.
20.	하늘은 매우 춥다.	It is very _____ in the sky.
21.	닉과 그의 친구들은 서로 껴안는다.	Nick and his friends hug _____.
22.	그들은 얼어서 눈이 된다.	They _____ and become snow.
23.	그때, 닉은 다시 사람으로 바뀐다.	At that moment, Nick changes into a _____ again.
24.	"와! 멋졌어!"	"Wow! That was so _____!"

A 빈칸에 어울리는 단어를 고르세요.

1. Which color is better? Yellow _____ blue?
   ① owl   ② oil   ③ or   ④ okay

2. Friends like to hug _____.
   ① each the other   ② each other   ③ each person   ④ each day

3. The _____ of my book is missing.
   ① chalk   ② color   ③ cooler   ④ cover

4. First, turn on the oven and _____ it to 180℃.
   ① heat   ② hit   ③ hat   ④ hot

5. The ocean can't _____ over.
   ① fry   ② freedom   ③ frozen   ④ freeze

6. The scientists found something on the _____ of Mars.
   ① surprise   ② surface   ③ suffer   ④ success

7. The river never stops; it always _____.
   ① flowers   ② floors   ③ flows   ④ floats

8. The water evaporates and turns into _____.
   ① waterfront   ② waterfall   ③ water pool   ④ water vapor

9. Tomorrow, it'll be cooler than today, so it will be _____.
   ① child   ② chili   ③ chiller   ④ chilly

10. An outgoing girl has _____ friends.
    ① a little   ② a lot   ③ after   ④ a lot of

11. The _____ is the movement of water.
    ① water cycle   ② water site   ③ water cyclone   ④ water city

12. A _____ is a human being.
   ① perfect ② person ③ perform ④ period

13. There are five _____ : the Pacific, Atlantic, Indian, Arctic, and Antarctic.
   ① options ② olives ③ occupations ④ oceans

14. A tadpole _____ a frog.
   ① takes in ② turns into ③ turns on ④ turns off

15. _____ fall down from the ceiling.
   ① Water drops ② Water cycle ③ Water rates ④ Water proof

16. This summer is too hot, so I hope this fall will be _____.
   ① cool ② call ③ coal ④ coil

B 밑줄 친 단어와 비슷한 뜻을 가진 단어를 고르세요.

17. The water from the mountain flows into the river.
   ① stake ② street ③ stream ④ station

18. The form of clouds looks like a sheep.
   ① fight ② figure ③ family ④ face

19. When water evaporates, it changes its form.
   ① wets ② fries ③ dries ④ cries

C 밑줄 친 단어와 반대되는 뜻을 가진 단어를 고르세요.

20. A little spider went up the wall.
   ① side ② down ③ upside ④ along

Score: _____ /20

Unit 6

About Junk Food

Word Check

A 다음 단어들의 우리말 뜻을 모두 알고 있나요? 확인해 보세요.

단어의 품사에 맞는 우리말 뜻을 쓰세요.

1. ☐ movie 〔명〕

2. ☐ test 〔동〕 〔명〕

3. ☐ as 〔전〕 〔접〕

4. ☐ meal 〔명〕

5. ☐ offer 〔동〕

6. ☐ limit 〔동〕 〔명〕

7. ☐ distance 〔명〕

8. ☐ treatment 〔명〕

9. ☐ throw up 〔구〕

10. ☐ weight 〔명〕

11. ☐ depression 〔명〕

12. ☐ quit 〔동〕

13. ☐ today 〔부〕

14. ☐ way 〔명〕 〔부〕

15. ☐ snatch 〔동〕

16. ☐ hate 〔동〕 〔명〕

17. ☐ woman 〔명〕

18. ☐ fresh 〔형〕

19. ☐ already 〔부〕

20. ☐ fall under a spell 〔구〕

21. ☐ regret 〔동〕

22. ☐ friendship 〔명〕

23. ☐ remove 〔동〕

24. ☐ human 〔명〕

B 우리말과 같은 뜻이 되도록 빈칸을 채워 영어 문장을 완성하세요.

1.	모건 스펄록은 '수퍼 사이즈 미'라는 영화를 만들었다.	Morgan Spurlock made the _____ *Super Size Me*.
2.	그는 스스로 패스트푸드의 악영향들을 시험했다.	He _____ the bad effects of fast food on himself.
3.	그는 다음과 같은 프로그램을 실행했다.	He carried out a program _____ follows.

4.	그는 패스트푸드점에서 하루 세끼를 먹었다.	He ate three _____ a day at a fast-food restaurant.
5.	음식점 종업원이 음식을 특대로 하는 것을 제안했다.	A restaurant worker _____ to supersize the meal.
6.	그는 걷는 것을 하루에 1~2 킬로미터로 제한했다.	He _____ himself to walking 1~2 km a day.
7.	그것은 미국인들이 매일 걷는 평균 거리이다.	That is the average _____ Americans walk daily.
8.	그는 규칙적으로 의사에게 치료를 받았다.	He got _____ from a doctor regularly.
9.	그는 패스트푸드를 먹은 4일 뒤에 토했다.	He _____ after eating fast food 4 days later.
10.	그의 몸무게는 한 달만에 85 킬로그램에서 96 킬로그램으로 증가했다.	His _____ increased from 85 kg to 96 kg in a month.
11.	그는 또 우울증과 고혈압 증상을 보였다.	He also got symptoms of _____ and high blood pressure.
12.	그는 패스트푸드를 먹는 것을 그만둬야 했다.	He had to _____ eating fast food.
13.	닉은 오늘 기분이 좋지 않았다.	Nick didn't feel well _____.
14.	닉과 매튜는 집에 오는 길에 버거를 먹고 있었다.	Nick and Matthew were eating burgers on their _____ home.
15.	닉은 더 먹기 위해 매튜의 버거를 낚아챘다.	Nick _____ Matthew's burger to eat some more.
16.	"너 정말 나쁘구나. 난 네가 싫어!"	"You're so bad. I _____ you!"
17.	어느 늙은 여자가 그녀의 과일 바구니를 그들 앞에 떨어뜨렸다.	An old _____ dropped her fruit basket in front of them.
18.	그녀는 그들에게 신선한 과일을 좀 주었다.	She gave them some _____ fruit.
19.	그들은 이미 버거가 되어 있었다.	They had _____ become burgers.
20.	닉과 매튜는 싸움 때문에 주문에 걸렸다.	Nick and Matthew _____ _____ because of their fight.
21.	그들이 싸운 것을 후회했을 때, 늙은 여자가 나타났다.	When they _____ fighting, the old woman appeared.
22.	그녀는 그들의 우정이 여전히 강하다고 확신했다.	She made sure that their _____ was still strong.
23.	그래서 그녀는 주문을 풀어주었다.	So she _____ the spell.
24.	그들은 다시 인간으로 변했다.	They changed back into _____ again.

Review Test

A 빈칸에 어울리는 단어를 고르세요.

1. I took the final _____. It was pretty hard.
   ① team   ② tear   ③ tree   ④ test

2. The ticket price is very expensive. But it includes a _____.
   ① meaning   ② meeting   ③ meal   ④ men

3. This road has a speed _____. You can't drive over 60 km/hr.
   ① life   ② lift   ③ list   ④ limit

4. The shopping mall is a long _____ from here. It's outside the city.
   ① dinosaur   ② diving   ③ distance   ④ dice

5. The soldiers can't get proper _____. There are not enough doctors in the hospital.
   ① treatment   ② trade   ③ travel   ④ twist

6. I feel like _____. I need to go to the toilet.
   ① taking a bath ② throwing up   ③ throwing out   ④ taking part in

7. _____ makes people feel blue. It's a mental disease.
   ① Direction   ② Danger   ③ Dream   ④ Depression

8. _____ is Monday. Tomorrow is Tuesday.
   ① Tonight   ② Today   ③ Together   ④ Toward

9. When you find the same card as this, _____ it.
   ① spell   ② stand   ③ swim   ④ snatch

10. I failed the exam. I _____ not having studied harder.
    ① reuse   ② refill   ③ reply   ④ regret

11. We're best friends. Our _____ will last forever.
    ① feed   ② friendship   ③ fire   ④ feeling

12. Would you _____ the toys on the floor? It's so messy.
① restart   ② remove   ③ remain   ④ recover

13. I don't like eating insects. I _____ them.
① help   ② hang   ③ have   ④ hate

14. I want to breathe _____ air. The air in this city is so polluted.
① fresh   ② frozen   ③ final   ④ falling

15. The train _____ left for Busan. You should change your ticket.
① already   ② all right   ③ alone   ④ almost

B 밑줄 친 단어와 비슷한 뜻을 가진 단어를 고르세요.

16. I watched a <u>movie</u> at 8:30 in the morning.
① four   ② fire   ③ film   ④ feeling

17. She <u>offers</u> me a chance to see a movie with her.
① supposes   ② supplies   ③ supports   ④ suggests

18. I will <u>quit</u> my job. I'm moving to Paris.
① give   ② give up   ③ get   ④ get up

19. Every <u>human</u> makes mistakes.
① person   ② power   ③ prince   ④ pepper

C 밑줄 친 단어와 반대되는 뜻을 가진 단어를 고르세요.

20. A <u>woman</u> is walking toward me now.
① mom   ② man   ③ mall   ④ mop

Score: _____ /20

The Seven Stars

Word Check

A 다음 단어들의 우리말 뜻을 모두 알고 있나요? 확인해 보세요.

단어의 품사에 맞는 우리말 뜻을 쓰세요.

1. ☐ northern (형)
2. ☐ almost (부)
3. ☐ constellation (명)
4. ☐ describe (동)
5. ☐ ox (명)
6. ☐ wagon (명)
7. ☐ bowl (명)
8. ☐ sailor (명)
9. ☐ direction (명)
10. ☐ position (명)
11. ☐ round (형)
12. ☐ once (부)

13. ☐ night (명)
14. ☐ southern (형)
15. ☐ boastful (형)
16. ☐ bother (동)
17. ☐ coward (명)
18. ☐ leave (동) (명)
19. ☐ alone (형) (부)
20. ☐ bite (동)
21. ☐ attack (동) (명)
22. ☐ sword (명)
23. ☐ opposite (형)
24. ☐ never (부)

B 우리말과 같은 뜻이 되도록 빈칸을 채워 영어 문장을 완성하세요.

1.	북쪽 하늘의 별무리를 보라.	Look at the group of stars in the _____ part of the sky.
2.	거의 모든 사람들이 일곱 개의 밝은 별 한 무리를 찾을 수 있다.	_____ everybody can find seven bright stars in a group.
3.	그것들은 세 번째로 큰 별자리를 형성한다.	They form the third largest _____ .

4.	고대 그리스인들은 그것을 긴 꼬리를 가진 곰이라고 묘사했다.	The ancient Greeks _____ it as a bear with a long tail.
5.	로마인들은 그 별들이 일곱 마리의 황소처럼 보인다고 믿었다.	The Romans believed that the stars looked like seven _____.
6.	바이킹들은 그것을 하늘을 여행하는 마차라고 생각했다.	The Vikings thought it was a _____ traveling in the sky.
7.	북미 원주민들은 그것이 그릇처럼 보인다고 말했다.	The native Americans said it looked like a _____.
8.	옛날 뱃사람들이 길을 잃었다.	Ancient _____ lost their way.
9.	북두칠성이 그들을 올바른 방향으로 안내해주었다.	The Big Dipper guided them in the right _____.
10.	그들은 북두칠성의 위치를 보고 시간을 분간할 수 있었다.	They could tell the time by looking at the _____ of the Big Dipper.
11.	그것은 나타나서 북극성 둘레를 돈다.	It appears to circle _____ the North star.
12.	그것은 북극성을 하룻밤에 한 번 돈다.	It circles Polaris _____ a night.
13.	그것은 어느 여름 밤에 일어났다.	It happened one summer _____.
14.	닉은 남쪽 하늘을 올려다본다.	Nick looks up at the _____ sky.
15.	오리온은 잘생겼지만 잘난 척하는 별이다.	Orion is a handsome but _____ star.
16.	그는 항상 다른 별들을 괴롭히고 작은 별들을 놀린다.	He always _____ the other stars and teases the small stars.
17.	"너는 겁쟁이야. 네 개는 웃기게 생겼어."	"You are a _____. Your dog looks funny."
18.	"그냥 떠나. 저리 가."	"Just _____. Go away."
19.	그는 혼자이다.	He is _____.
20.	닉의 개는 으르렁거리며 오리온을 물려고 달려든다.	Nick's dog growls and rushes to _____ Orion.
21.	오리온이 우리를 공격한다.	Orion _____ us.
22.	그는 칼과 방패를 가지고 있다.	He has a _____ and a shield.
23.	전갈과 오리온은 반대쪽 하늘에 놓인다.	The scorpion and Orion are placed on _____ sides of the sky.
24.	그들은 밤하늘에서 다시는 만나지 않았다.	They have _____ met again in the night sky.

Review Test

A 빈칸에 어울리는 단어를 고르세요.

1. He has a _____. He looks like a soldier.
   ① swing   ② switch   ③ sweet   ④ sword

2. Look at the bright _____. It's a scorpion.
   ① constellation   ② coin   ③ credit   ④ contact

3. The train just arrived. It's time to _____.
   ① lead   ② leave   ③ learn   ④ leaf

4. Can you _____ what he looked like?
   ① decide   ② describe   ③ design   ④ develop

5. You're going the wrong way. It's _____ of the bank.
   ① optional   ② opportunity   ③ opposite   ④ opening

6. Don't be scared. This dog doesn't _____.
   ① bear   ② begin   ③ become   ④ bite

7. I'm cold. A _____ of hot soup, please.
   ① ball   ② bowl   ③ owl   ④ howl

8. I play computer games _____ a week. That's enough for me.
   ① one   ② over   ③ once   ④ only

9. You can't go north. You need to change _____.
   ① diamond   ② direction   ③ difficulty   ④ dictation

10. What is your _____ in the company?
    ① position   ② point   ③ police   ④ power

11. He is honest. He _____ tells lies.
    ① nature   ② ever   ③ never   ④ news

12. Don't _____ me. Just read the book quietly.
    ① bathe   ② believe   ③ brother   ④ bother

13. She has a _____ face. She is cute.
    ① round   ② found   ③ pound   ④ bound

14. I'm not a _____. I'm brave and strong.
    ① cowboy   ② coward   ③ channel   ④ cone

15. He loves the sea. He will become a _____.
    ① safety   ② sample   ③ salesman   ④ sailor

B 밑줄 친 단어와 비슷한 뜻을 가진 단어를 고르세요.

16. It's <u>almost</u> ten o'clock. It's time to go to bed.
    ① never   ② nearly   ③ hardly   ④ little

17. She can't stay <u>alone</u>. I will stay with her.
    ① partly   ② lonely   ③ evenly   ④ calmly

C 밑줄 친 단어와 반대되는 뜻을 가진 단어를 고르세요.

18. The wolf <u>attacks</u> the dog. The dog doesn't fight back.
    ① raises   ② saves   ③ offers   ④ defends

19. I can't sleep at <u>night</u>. I'm very tired.
    ① afternoon   ② bed   ③ day   ④ time

20. He's very <u>boastful</u>. I don't like him.
    ① proud   ② talkative   ③ humble   ④ terrible

Score: _____ /20

Unit 8

Famous Places

Word Check

A 다음 단어들의 우리말 뜻을 모두 알고 있나요? 확인해 보세요.

> 단어의 품사에 맞는 우리말 뜻을 쓰세요.

1. ☐ discover	동		13. ☐ field trip	명	
2. ☐ statue	명		14. ☐ exhibition	명	
3. ☐ carve	동		15. ☐ exit	명	동
4. ☐ number	명		16. ☐ black out	구	
5. ☐ and	접		17. ☐ loud	형	
6. ☐ bottom	명		18. ☐ mummy	명	
7. ☐ how	부		19. ☐ scared	형	
8. ☐ heavy	형		20. ☐ occur	동	
9. ☐ research	명 동		21. ☐ come up to	구	
10. ☐ sleigh	명		22. ☐ speak	동	
11. ☐ attractive	형		23. ☐ watch	동 명	
12. ☐ heritage	명		24. ☐ backward	부	

B 우리말과 같은 뜻이 되도록 빈칸을 채워 영어 문장을 완성하세요.

1.	이스터 섬은 1722년 일요일이었던 부활절에 발견되었다.	Easter Island was _____ on Easter Sunday in 1722.
2.	이곳은 모아이라는 커다란 석상들로 유명하다.	It is famous for the large stone _____ called moai.
3.	그것들 대부분은 몸이 보이게 조각되었다.	Most of them are _____ to show a body.

4.	그것들 중 적은 수만이 몸 전체를 보여준다.	Only a small _____ of them show a complete body.
5.	조각상들의 높이는 1 미터에서 30 미터까지이고, 무게는 각각 거의 20톤에 이른다.	The height of the _____ ranges from 1 m to 30 m, _____ they weigh almost 20 tons each.
6.	그것들의 아랫 부분은 땅에 숨겨져 있다.	Their _____ are hidden in the ground.
7.	사람들이 어떻게 그것들을 움직였는지 유추해 볼 수 있는가?	Can you guess _____ people moved them?
8.	그것들은 너무 무거워서 사람들이 움직이기 어려웠다.	They were so _____ that it was difficult for people to move them.
9.	조사에 의하면 많은 야자수가 있었다.	_____ shows there were lots of palm trees.
10.	그래서 사람들은 그것들을 움직일 수 있게 야자수로 썰매를 만들 수 있었다.	So people could have made _____ out of the palm trees to move them.
11.	모아이는 아주 매력적이다.	The moai are so _____ .
12.	많은 관광객들이 세계 유산인 모아이를 보기 위해 방문한다.	Many tourists visit to see the world _____ , moai.
13.	닉은 박물관으로 현장 학습을 갔다.	Nick went on a _____ to the museum.
14.	그는 고대 이집트 전시실에 혼자 남겨졌다.	He was left alone in the ancient Egypt _____ room.
15.	그는 출구를 찾으려 했지만 넘어졌다.	He tried to find the _____ , but he fell down.
16.	그가 넘어졌을 때, 박물관에서 기절했다.	When he fell down, he _____ in the museum.
17.	벽이 큰 소리를 내더니 움직이기 시작했다.	The wall made a _____ sound and began to move.
18.	닉은 미라들을 보고 놀랐다.	Nick was surprised to see _____ .
19.	그는 무서워서 도망쳤다.	He got _____ and ran away.
20.	그가 뒤를 돌아봤을 때, 놀라운 일이 일어났다.	When he looked back, a surprising thing _____ .
21.	그것들이 사라지고 파라오가 닉에게 다가 왔다.	They disappeared and a Pharaoh _____ _____ Nick.
22.	파라오가 닉에게 말했다.	The Pharaoh _____ to Nick.
23.	"조심해라, 내 새로운 병사여, 이리로 오거라."	" _____ out, my new soldier. Come here."
24.	그 순간, 닉이 뒤로 물러났다.	At that moment, Nick stepped _____ .

Review Test

빈칸에 어울리는 단어를 고르세요.

1. A woman is speaking in a _____ voice. It's annoying.
   ① lifted   ② loud   ③ like   ④ light

2. The _____ of Liberty is in New York. It's a symbol of freedom.
   ① State   ② Statue   ③ Start   ④ Street

3. When the ghost suddenly _____ me, I was scared.
   ① came true   ② came across   ③ came up to   ④ came up with

4. The _____ of people in South Korea is about fifty million.
   ① nature   ② number   ③ need   ④ nurse

5. This table is too _____. Would you help me move it?
   ① hear   ② hurt   ③ heavy   ④ high

6. Can you _____ English? I don't understand Japanese.
   ① spring   ② send   ③ stand   ④ speak

7. I enjoy taking a _____ ride down the hill. That's why I like winter.
   ① sleigh   ② skirt   ③ show   ④ swimming

8. Did you _____ the TV show? My favorite actor was in it.
   ① wait   ② water   ③ win   ④ watch

9. On April 24, the 6th graders went on a _____. They visited the national museum.
   ① final exam   ② field trip   ③ field time   ④ four times

10. My first _____ was successful. Lots of people attended.
    ① exercise   ② example   ③ explain   ④ exhibition

11. Every building has to have emergency _____. They are very important.
    ① exits   ② elephants   ③ environment   ④ earth

12. Seoul has lots of _____ sites. Many foreigners visit them.
    ① height   ② heritage   ③ head   ④ health

13. Columbus _____ America in 1492. Before that, America was unknown.
    ① disguised   ② discovered   ③ discussed   ④ discouraged

14. I _____ traveling in Japan on the Internet.
    ① reported   ② researched   ③ revised   ④ restored

15. A famous artist _____ that statue. It's *The Thinker* by Rodin.
    ① cared   ② colored   ③ could   ④ carved

B 밑줄 친 단어와 비슷한 뜻을 가진 단어를 고르세요.

16. He is so underline{attractive}.
    ① classic   ② clear   ③ charming   ④ clean

17. This movie makes me scared.
    ① awake   ② afraid   ③ available   ④ asleep

18. Many traffic accidents occur at this intersection.
    ① hurt   ② have   ③ happen   ④ hang

C 밑줄 친 단어와 반대되는 뜻을 가진 단어를 고르세요.

19. Look at the bottom of the page.
    ① top   ② tower   ③ test   ④ tank

20. He can dance backward.
    ① together   ② tomorrow   ③ today   ④ forward

Score: _____ /20

A Mysterious Plant

Word Check

A 다음 단어들의 우리말 뜻을 모두 알고 있나요? 확인해 보세요.

> 단어의 품사에 맞는 우리말 뜻을 쓰세요.

1. ☐ mysterious 형 _____
2. ☐ unlike 전 _____
3. ☐ nutrient 명 _____
4. ☐ poor 형 _____
5. ☐ endanger 동 _____
6. ☐ greenhouse 명 _____
7. ☐ wide 부 _____ 형 _____
8. ☐ short 형 _____
9. ☐ crawl 동 _____
10. ☐ allow 동 _____
11. ☐ digest 동 _____
12. ☐ if 접 _____

13. ☐ gather 동 _____
14. ☐ get rid of 구 _____
15. ☐ troublesome 형 _____
16. ☐ solution 명 _____
17. ☐ key 명 _____ 형 _____
18. ☐ swamp 명 _____
19. ☐ lose one's footing 구 _____
20. ☐ side 명 _____
21. ☐ tickle 동 _____
22. ☐ die 동 _____
23. ☐ shovel 명 _____
24. ☐ helpful 형 _____

B 우리말과 같은 뜻이 되도록 빈칸을 채워 영어 문장을 완성하세요.

1.	파리지옥은 신비로운 식물이다.	The Venus flytrap is a _____ plant.
2.	다른 식물들과는 달리 이것은 곤충을 잡아먹는 식물이다.	_____ other plants, it is an insect-eating plant.
3.	이것은 개미와 같은 곤충들을 잡아먹으며 영양분들을 섭취한다.	It gets _____ from eating insects like ants.

4.	파리지옥은 척박한 조건에서 산다.	The Venus flytrap lives in _____ conditions.
5.	사람들이 너무 많은 파리지옥을 채집해서 그것들이 위험에 처하게 되었다.	People collect so many Venus flytraps that they have become _____.
6.	그래서 그것들은 오늘날 온실들에서 길러진다.	So they are grown in _____ today.
7.	파리지옥의 잎들은 보통 활짝 열려 있다.	The leaves of the Venus flytrap are usually open _____.
8.	짧은 털들이 잎을 덮고 있다.	_____ hairs cover the leaves.
9.	곤충이 잎 위를 기어 다니면 잎들이 재빨리 잎을 닫는다.	When an insect _____ on its leaves, its leaves close quickly.
10.	털들과 잎들은 곤충이 탈출하는 것을 허용하지 않는다.	The hairs and leaves don't _____ the insect to escape.
11.	파리지옥은 곤충의 부드러운 안쪽 부분을 소화한다.	The Venus flytrap _____ the soft, inner parts of the insect.
12.	만약 그것이 돌을 삼키면 잎들은 다시 잎을 연다.	_____ it swallows a stone, the leaves reopen.
13.	닉과 그의 친구들이 미셸의 집에 모인다.	Nick and his friends _____ at Michelle's house.
14.	"어떻게 이 초파리들을 없앨 수 있을까?"	"How can we _____ _____ these fruit flies?"
15.	"이것들은 골칫덩어리야."	"They're _____."
16.	"나에게 해결책이 있어."	"I have a _____."
17.	"파리지옥이 바로 그 비결이지."	"A Venus flytrap is the _____."
18.	그들은 파리지옥이 사는 늪으로 간다.	They go to a _____ where the Venus flytrap grows.
19.	그 순간, 그는 발을 헛디뎌 미끄러진다.	At that moment, he _____ and slips.
20.	"잎의 양쪽을 잡아당겨."	"Pull the _____ of the leaves."
21.	"내가 이것을 간질일게." 라고 저스틴이 말한다.	"I'm going to _____ it," says Justin.
22.	닉이 말한다. "휴~! 거의 죽을 뻔했어."	"Whew~! I almost _____," says Nick.
23.	그들은 삽으로 그것을 파낸다.	They dig it out with a _____.
24.	정말 유용한 식물이다!	What a _____ plant!

Review Test

A 빈칸에 어울리는 단어를 고르세요.

1. We _____ at my grandparents' house on New Year's Day.
   ① together   ② gather   ③ locate   ④ get

2. The tiger was 29 years old. He _____ yesterday.
   ① died   ② allowed   ③ dead   ④ digested

3. What is the _____ sentence in the story?
   ① side   ② key   ③ wide   ④ knee

4. Children love _____ and interesting stories.
   ① mistakes   ② miss   ③ mysterious   ④ mass

5. We can grow many vegetables in a _____ in winter.
   ① green   ② box   ③ bag   ④ greenhouse

6. When I _____ my baby brother, he always laughs.
   ① ticket   ② tickle   ③ take   ④ time

7. Global warming _____ our lives. It's really serious.
   ① endangers   ② enable   ③ enough   ④ saves

8. Thank you. Your advice was _____ to me.
   ① wasteful   ② useless   ③ helpful   ④ careful

9. My uncle can _____ rocks. It's incredible.
   ① different   ② swamp   ③ shovel   ④ digest

10. My father _____ me to go camping with my friends.
    ① allowed   ② got rid of   ③ lost his footing   ④ crawled

11. During my vacation, I got bitten by mosquitoes. They are so
    _____.
    ① mistakes   ② sick   ③ troublesome   ④ side

12. Whenever I ask my mom for some help, she tells me to find
    the _____ by myself.
    ① solve   ② serious   ③ problem   ④ solution

13. Milk has some _____, so we have to drink it every day.
 ① introduce ② nature ③ nutrients ④ nurse

14. When I was six months old, I started _____.
 ① reading ② running ③ studying ④ crawling

15. _____ I were a teacher, I wouldn't give any homework to students.
 ① In ② As ③ If ④ On

B 밑줄 친 단어와 비슷한 뜻을 가진 단어를 고르세요.

16. There is too much trash. We have to <u>get rid of</u> the trash.
 ① remove ② get to ③ get into ④ result

17. The school <u>allows</u> the students to study until 8 p.m.
 ① limits ② admits ③ leaves ④ applies

C 밑줄 친 단어와 반대되는 뜻을 가진 단어를 고르세요.

18. Bill is <u>rich</u>. So he can buy anything he wants.
 ① poor ② important ③ possible ④ reasonable

19. I swim very well <u>like</u> a fish. So I will become a swimmer.
 ① same ② as ③ look ④ unlike

20. Elephants' trunks are so <u>long</u>. They use their trunks to pick up food.
 ① wide ② big ③ short ④ small

Score: _____ /20

The Guinness Book

Word Check

A 다음 단어들의 우리말 뜻을 모두 알고 있나요? 확인해 보세요.

> 단어의 품사에 맞는 우리말 뜻을 쓰세요.

1. ☐ huge (형)
2. ☐ the same ~ as ... (구)
3. ☐ cockroach (명)
4. ☐ measure (동)
5. ☐ who (대)
6. ☐ dwarf (명)
7. ☐ fact (명)
8. ☐ detail (동) (명)
9. ☐ break a record (구)
10. ☐ apply (동)
11. ☐ send (동)
12. ☐ now (부)

13. ☐ beef (명)
14. ☐ upset (형) (동)
15. ☐ medicine (명)
16. ☐ chalk (명)
17. ☐ in class (구)
18. ☐ button up (구)
19. ☐ blame (동)
20. ☐ fall off (구)
21. ☐ tie (명) (동)
22. ☐ sore (형)
23. ☐ disappoint (동)
24. ☐ continue (동)

B 우리말과 같은 뜻이 되도록 빈칸을 채워 영어 문장을 완성하세요.

1.	세계에서 가장 거대한 피자는 얼마나 클까?	How big is the _____ pizza in the world?
2.	그것은 10층 높이 건물과 같은 크기이다.	That is _____ size _____ a 10-story building.
3.	세계에서 가장 작은 바퀴벌레는 얼마나 작을까?	How small is the smallest _____ in the world?

4.	그것은 9 밀리미터였다.	It 9 mm long.
5.	세계에서 가장 가벼운 사람은 누굴까?	is the world's lightest person?
6.	그는 멕시코 난쟁이로 67 센티미터의 키에 2.14 킬로그램이다.	It is a Mexican , who is 67 cm tall and weighs 2.14 kg.
7.	우리는 이러한 사실들을 세계 기록 기네스북에서 찾을 수 있다.	We can find these in the Guinness Book of World Records.
8.	이것은 세계의 새로운 기록들을 상세하게 보여 주는 인기 있는 책이다.	It is a popular book that the world's new records.
9.	세계 기록을 깨고 싶은 사람이 있는가?	Does anyone want to world ?
10.	시도해 보고 기네스 세계 기록에 신청해라.	Try and then for a Guinness world record.
11.	당신의 새로운 기록을 기네스북에 보내라.	your new record to the Guinness book.
12.	지금 해봐라.	Try it .
13.	닉은 소고기 최대한 빨리 먹기를 시도한다.	Nick tries eating as fast as he can.
14.	그는 배탈이 난다.	He has an stomach.
15.	그래서 그는 약을 좀 먹는다.	So he takes some .
16.	닉은 분필을 최대한 멀리 던지는 연습을 한다.	Nick practices throwing as far as he can.
17.	그는 수업 중에 그것을 던져서 선생님께 혼이 난다.	He gets punished by his teacher for throwing it .
18.	닉은 옷 단추 빨리 잠그기를 해본다.	Nick tries to his clothes quickly.
19.	그의 엄마는 그를 혼낸다.	His mom him.
20.	왜냐하면 그의 옷의 모든 단추들이 떨어져서이다.	Because all of the buttons on his clothes .
21.	그는 신발 끈을 가장 빨리 묶는 것을 해본다.	He tries to his shoes the fastest.
22.	그는 손이 아파서 포기한다.	He gives up because his hands are .
23.	닉은 정말 실망한다. 하지만 닉은 결코 포기하지 않는다.	Nick's really . But Nick never gives up.
24.	닉은 세계 기록을 세우려고 계속 시도할 것이다.	Nick will to try to set a world record.

Review Test

A 빈칸에 어울리는 단어를 고르세요.

1. Don't put off what you have to do today. Do it _____.
   ① no   ② nor   ③ now   ④ none

2. A long time ago, there were _____ animals. They were called mammoths.
   ① hug   ② huge   ③ hot   ④ hut

3. To _____ a letter is an old form of communication.
   ① sand   ② send   ③ sale   ④ sent

4. A teacher writes a sentence on the board with _____.
   ① chair   ② change   ③ chart   ④ chalk

5. I don't know him. _____ is he?
   ① Why   ② What   ③ When   ④ Who

6. She waits for her mom, but her mom doesn't come. She is _____.
   ① disappointed ② disappeared ③ disapproved ④ disagreed

7. I will _____ for a scholarship to Harvard University.
   ① play   ② apply   ③ apple   ④ reapply

8. She gets a cold. She has a _____ throat.
   ① sore   ② soil   ③ sort   ④ sorry

9. The painter is famous for painting in great _____. His pictures look very realistic.
   ① detect   ② describe   ③ decide   ④ detail

10. The player wants to set a new record. She needs to _____.
    ① break a window ② break a record ③ break a bone ④ break a recovery

11. My baby is afraid of your dog. Can you _____ it up?
    ① tie   ② till   ③ tired   ④ tight

12. A _____ is a kind of bug. It lives everywhere.
　① peacock　　　② cockroach　　　③ cocktail　　　④ coating

13. How can I _____ my desk? Can I use my ruler?
　① meat　　　② messenger　　　③ master　　　④ measure

14. I could put on and _____ my clothes by myself when I was 7 years old.
　① butter up　　　② button up　　　③ beat up　　　④ buttonhole

15. He teased his sister. She was _____ and shouted at him.
　① upset　　　② upper　　　③ upon　　　④ upstairs

B 밑줄 친 단어와 비슷한 뜻을 가진 단어를 고르세요.

16. I will <u>continue</u> to study hard next year.
　① go　　　② grow　　　③ go on　　　④ gather

17. Tell me the <u>facts</u>! What happened yesterday?
　① trees　　　② truth　　　③ trains　　　④ tries

18. Even though you have a bad cold, don't take too much <u>medicine</u>.
　① pall　　　② pull　　　③ pill　　　④ poll

C 밑줄 친 단어와 반대되는 뜻을 가진 단어를 고르세요.

19. Have you ever seen a <u>dwarf</u>?
　① backyard　　　② giant　　　③ front　　　④ along

20. My mom never <u>blames</u> me. She is very kind.
　① prides　　　② pleases　　　③ places　　　④ praises

Score: ____ /20

• Answers •

Unit 1 Personality   p.2

Word Check

Ⓐ 1. 모든 사람, 모두   2. 성격, 개성
3. 부끄러워 하는, 수줍은   4. 조심성 있는
5. 실용적인, 현실적인   6. 초점을 맞추다; 초점
7. 목표, 결승점   8. 끝   9. 사회적인, 사교적인
10. 포기하다   11. 양쪽의
12. 책임이 있는, 책임감 있는   13. 반 친구, 급우
14. 끔찍한, 지독한, 무서운   15. 이기적인   16. 빌리다
17. 개구쟁이의, 장난이 심한   18. 대답하다; 대답
19. 놀리다, 괴롭히다   20. 불평하다
21. 좋아하다; ~ 같이, ~처럼   22. 아이, 어린이
23. 다른 것들, 다른 사람들   24. 거친, 힘든, 질긴

Ⓑ 1. Everyone   2. personality   3. shy   4. careful
5. practical   6. focus   7. goal   8. end   9. social
10. give up   11. both   12. responsible
13. classmates   14. awful   15. selfish
16. borrow   17. naughty   18. answer
19. teased   20. complains   21. like   22. kid
23. others   24. tough

Review Test

Ⓐ 1. ③   2. ②   3. ④   4. ③   5. ①   6. ②   7. ③
8. ②   9. ④   10. ④   11. ①   12. ②   13. ④
14. ②   15. ①

Ⓑ 16. ③   17. ②   18. ③

Ⓒ 19. ②   20. ④

Unit 2 A Swimming Race   p.6

Word Check

Ⓐ 1. 개최되다   2. 블록, 구역   3. ~라는 것; 저것; 저
4. 신호; 신호를 보내다   5. 힘차게, 강력하게
6. 최선을 다하다   7. 막상막하로, 비등하게
8. 예측하다   9. 결과, 결실   10. 따라잡다
11. 초; 두 번째의   12. 기록; 기록하다   13. 거북이

14. 달아나다   15. ~쪽으로, ~을 향해   16. ~보다
17. 첨벙거리다   18. 물장구치다   19. 쥐가 나다
20. 왼쪽의; 왼쪽   21. 더 이상   22. 구하다, 저장하다
23. 생명의 은인, 인명 구조자   24. 되돌아가다

Ⓑ 1. taking place   2. blocks   3. that   4. signal
5. powerfully   6. do their best   7. neck and neck
8. predict   9. results   10. catches up with
11. seconds   12. record   13. turtle   14. ran away
15. toward   16. than   17. splash   18. Paddle
19. got a cramp   20. left   21. anymore
22. saving   23. lifesaver   24. went back

Review Test

Ⓐ 1. ③   2. ①   3. ④   4. ④   5. ①   6. ②   7. ③
8. ④   9. ②   10. ①   11. ④   12. ②   13. ①
14. ②   15. ④

Ⓑ 16. ③   17. ②   18. ①   19. ④

Ⓒ 20. ③

Unit 3 The Tallest Building   p.10

Word Check

Ⓐ 1. 환영하다   2. 고층 빌딩, 마천루   3. 키가 큰, 높은
4. 높이, 키   5. 철   6. 강한   7. 회사   8. 백만; 백만의
9. 관찰   10. 흔들리다   11. 도시   12. 지평선
13. 토네이도, (강력한) 폭풍   14. ~ 안으로, ~ 속으로
15. 명령하다, 주문하다; 명령, 순서, 질서, 주문
16. 벽돌   17. 빨리   18. 하늘, 천국   19. 돌
20. 폭풍(우)   21. (건물 등이) 무너지다   22. 먼지
23. 마루, 층   24. 파괴하다, 멸망하다

Ⓑ 1. Welcome   2. skyscraper   3. tallest   4. height
5. steel   6. strong   7. companies   8. million
9. observation   10. sways   11. city   12. skyline
13. tornado   14. into   15. bricks   16. order
17. quickly   18. heaven   19. stones   20. storm
21. collapses   22. dust   23. floor   24. destroyed

Review Test

Ⓐ 1. ③ 2. ② 3. ② 4. ② 5. ④ 6. ② 7. ③
8. ③ 9. ② 10. ① 11. ① 12. ④ 13. ①
14. ④ 15. ③

Ⓑ 16. ② 17. ②

Ⓒ 18. ④ 19. ③ 20. ③

Unit 4 Paper World   p.14

Word Check

Ⓐ 1. 습지대 2. 고대의 3. 하나도 없는, ~도 없는; 아니
4. 전에 5. 부분 6. 가늘고 긴 조각; (껍질 등을) 벗기다
7. 적시다, 담그다 8. 그 때에, 그 다음에
9. (종이) 한 장, 시트 10. 햇빛 11. 기원, 유래
12. 세기, 100년 13. 미술 수업
14. 스케치; 스케치하다 15. 지우다 16. 빛을 내다
17. 모든 것 18. 깨닫다 19. 도화지 20. 듣다
21. 흔들다; 파도, 파장 22. 좌우를 둘러보다
23. 문지르다, 비비다 24. 튀어나오다

Ⓑ 1. wetlands 2. ancient 3. no 4. ago
5. part 6. part, strips 7. soaked 8. Then
9. sheets 10. sunlight 11. origin 12. century
13. art class 14. sketching 15. erases
16. gives out light 17. Everything 18. realizes
19. drawing paper 20. looks around 21. Listen
22. waves 23. rubs 24. pops out

Review Test

Ⓐ 1. ③ 2. ② 3. ① 4. ④ 5. ② 6. ① 7. ①
8. ② 9. ③ 10. ④ 11. ④ 12. ② 13. ①
14. ② 15. ③ 16. ②

Ⓑ 17. ③ 18. ② 19. ③

Ⓒ 20. ④

Unit 5 Water Changes   p.18

Word Check

Ⓐ 1. 표면, 평면 2. (큰) 강 3. 열; 뜨겁게 하다
4. 수증기 5. 일어서다, 올라가다 6. 위로 7. 물방울
8. 모습, 형태; 형성하다 9. 또는, 혹은 10. 흐르다
11. 아래로 12. 물의 순환
13. 뚜껑, 표지, 덮개; 덮다, 감추다, 포함하다
14. 양 15. 바다 16. 가벼워지다, 가볍게 해주다
17. 변하다 18. 증발하다, 사라지다 19. 많은
20. 차가운, 냉담한, 추운 21. 서로
22. 얼게 하다, 움직이지 않다 23. 사람
24. 멋진, 시원한

Ⓑ 1. surface 2. river 3. heats 4. water vapor
5. rises 6. up 7. water drops 8. form 9. or
10. down 11. flow 12. water cycle
13. covered 14. sheep 15. ocean 16. lighten
17. turns into 18. evaporates, up 19. a lot of
20. chilly 21. each other 22. freeze 23. person
24. cool

Review Test

Ⓐ 1. ③ 2. ② 3. ④ 4. ① 5. ④ 6. ② 7. ③
8. ④ 9. ④ 10. ④ 11. ① 12. ② 13. ④
14. ② 15. ① 16. ①

Ⓑ 17. ③ 18. ② 19. ③

Ⓒ 20. ②

Unit 6 About Junk Food   p.22

Word Check

Ⓐ 1. 영화 2. 시험하다, 검사하다; 시험
3. ~ 같이, ~처럼; ~ 하는 동안에, ~ 때문에
4. 식사 5. 제안하다, 제공하다 6. 제한하다; 제한
7. 거리 8. 치료 9. 토하다 10. 체중, 무게
11. 우울증 12. 그만두다 13. 오늘
14. 길, 방향, 방식; 훨씬 15. 잡아채다, 낚아채다
16. 몹시 싫어하다; 증오 17. 여자 18. 신선한
19. 이미, 벌써 20. 마법에 걸리다 21. 후회하다
22. 우정 23. 없애다, 제거하다 24. 사람, 인간

Ⓑ 1. movie 2. tested 3. as 4. meals 5. offered
6. limited 7. distance 8. treatment
9. threw up 10. weight 11. depression
12. quit 13. today 14. way 15. snatched
16. hate 17. woman 18. fresh 19. already
20. fell under a spell 21. regretted
22. friendship 23. removed 24. humans

Review Test

(A) 1. ④ 2. ③ 3. ④ 4. ③ 5. ① 6. ② 7. ④
8. ② 9. ④ 10. ④ 11. ② 12. ② 13. ④
14. ① 15. ①

(B) 16. ③ 17. ④ 18. ② 19. ①

(C) 20. ②

Unit 7 The Seven Stars p.26

Word Check

(A) 1. 북쪽의 2. 거의 3. 별자리 4. 묘사하다, 설명하다
5. 황소 6. 마차, 수레 7. 사발 8. 선원, 뱃사람
9. 방향, 지시 10. 위치 11. 둥근 12. 한 번 13. 밤
14. 남쪽의 15. 자랑하는, 허풍 떠는 16. 괴롭히다
17. 겁쟁이 18. 남기다, 떠나다, 맡기다; 휴가
19. 혼자의; 홀로 20. 물다 21. 공격하다; 공격, 폭행
22. 칼 23. 반대의 24. 결코 ~않다

(B) 1. northern 2. Almost 3. constellation
4. described 5. oxen 6. wagon 7. bowl
8. sailors 9. direction 10. position 11. round
12. once 13. night 14. southern 15. boastful
16. bothers 17. coward 18. leave 19. alone
20. bite 21. attacks 22. sword 23. opposite
24. never

Review Test

(A) 1. ④ 2. ① 3. ② 4. ② 5. ③ 6. ④ 7. ②
8. ③ 9. ② 10. ① 11. ③ 12. ④ 13. ①
14. ② 15. ④

(B) 16. ② 17. ②

(C) 18. ④ 19. ③ 20. ③

Unit 8 Famous Places p.30

Word Check

(A) 1. 발견하다 2. 조각상 3. 조각하다, 새기다 4. 수
5. 그리고 6. 아래 7. 어떻게
8. 무거운, (양·정도 등이) 많은(심한)
9. 연구, 조사; 연구하다 10. 썰매 11. 매력적인
12. 유산 13. 현장 학습 14. 전시 15. 출구; 나가다
16. 기절하다, 깜깜하게 만들다 17. 소리가 큰, 시끄러운
18. 미라 19. 겁먹은 20. 일어나다
21. 다가오다, (특정 지점까지) 오다 22. 말하다
23. 보다, (잠깐 동안) 봐주다, 조심하다; 손목시계
24. 뒤로

(B) 1. discovered 2. statues 3. carved 4. number
5. statues, and 6. bottoms 7. how 8. heavy
9. Research 10. sleighs 11. attractive
12. heritage 13. field trip 14. exhibition
15. exit 16. blacked out 17. loud
18. mummies 19. scared 20. occurred
21. came up to 22. spoke 23. Watch
24. backward

Review Test

(A) 1. ② 2. ② 3. ③ 4. ② 5. ③ 6. ④ 7. ①
8. ④ 9. ② 10. ④ 11. ① 12. ② 13. ②
14. ② 15. ④

(B) 16. ③ 17. ② 18. ③

(C) 19. ① 20. ④

Unit 9 A Mysterious Plant p.34

Word Check

(A) 1. 신비한, 불가사의한 2. ~와 다른 3. 영양소, 영양분
4. 빈약한, 가난한 5. 위험에 빠뜨리다 6. 온실
7. 활짝, 넓은 8. 짧은 9. 엎드려 기다
10. 허락하다, 인정하다 11. 소화하다
12. 만약 ~한다면 13. 모이다 14. ~을 없애다
15. 골칫거리인 16. 해결책, 해답
17. 비결, 열쇠; 가장 중요한, 핵심적인 18. 늪, 습지
19. 발을 헛디디다 20. 쪽, 면 21. 간질이다
22. 죽다 23. 삽 24. 도움이 되는

(B) 1. mysterious 2. Unlike 3. nutrients 4. poor
5. endangered 6. greenhouses 7. wide
8. Short 9. crawls 10. allow 11. digests
12. If 13. gather 14. get rid of 15. troublesome
16. solution 17. key 18. swamp
19. loses his footing 20. sides 21. tickle
22. died 23. shovel 24. helpful

Review Test

Ⓐ 1. ② 2. ① 3. ② 4. ③ 5. ④ 6. ② 7. ①
8. ③ 9. ④ 10. ① 11. ③ 12. ④ 13. ③
14. ④ 15. ③

Ⓑ 16. ① 17. ②

Ⓒ 18. ① 19. ④ 20. ③

Unit ⑩ The Guinness Book p.38

Word Check

Ⓐ 1. 거대한 2. …와 같은 ~ 3. 바퀴벌레
4. 재다, 측정하다, (길이 등이) ~이다 5. 누구
6. 난쟁이 7. 사실, 실제 8. 자세히 말하다; 자세한 설명
9. 기록을 깨다 10. 신청하다, 지원하다
11. (물건 등을) 보내다 12. 지금, 당장 13. 소고기
14. 속상한, (위 따위에) 탈이 난; 화나게 하다, 넘어뜨리다, 뒤집다 15. 약, 의약품 16. 분필 17. 수업 중인
18. 단추를 채워 잠그다, (입·지갑 등을) 꼭 잠그다
19. 혼내다, ~ 탓으로 돌리다 20. 떨어지다
21. 끈, 매듭; 묶다 22. 아픈, 슬픔에 잠긴
23. 실망시키다 24. 계속하다

Ⓑ 1. hugest 2. the same, as 3. cockroach
4. measured 5. Who 6. dwarf 7. facts
8. details 9. break a, record 10. apply
11. Send 12. now 13. beef 14. upset
15. medicine 16. chalk 17. in class
18. button up 19. blames 20. fall off 21. tie
22. sore 23. disappointed 24. continue

Review Test

Ⓐ 1. ③ 2. ② 3. ② 4. ④ 5. ④ 6. ① 7. ②
8. ① 9. ④ 10. ② 11. ① 12. ② 13. ④
14. ② 15. ①

Ⓑ 16. ③ 17. ② 18. ③

Ⓒ 19. ② 20. ④

Wow! Smart Grammar

전 3권 시리즈

스토리를 타고 흐르는 기본 핵심 영문법!

- ⭐ 흥미로운 **스토리**에 기반한 **생생한 예문**과 체계적인 연습문제
- ⭐ 다양한 유형의 **3단계 연습문제** Quiz Time
- ⭐ 중학교 시험·공인 영어 시험 대비도 OK! Review Test
- ⭐ 부담 없이 익히는 **영어권 문화 상식** Super Duper Fun Time
- ⭐ 스마트한 **자기주도학습의 파트너**, 워크북 & 휴대용 단어장
- ⭐ 책 속의 **영어문장 해석** 무료 다운로드 www.darakwon.co.kr

🦎 다락원